Australian
GEOGRAPHIC
SOUTH WEST AUSTRALIA
INCLUDING PERTH & MARGARET RIVER

By Simon Nevill

WOODSLANE
PRESS

Woodslane Press Pty Ltd
10 Apollo Street
Warriewood, NSW 2102
Email: info@woodslane.com.au
Tel: 02 8445 2300 Website: www.woodslane.com.au

First published in Australia in 2019 by Woodslane Press in association with Australian Geographic
© 2019 Woodslane Press, photographs © Australian Geographic and others
(see acknowledgements on page 62)

NATIONAL LIBRARY OF AUSTRALIA

A catalogue record for this book is available from the National Library of Australia

Printed in China by KS Printing
Cover image: Elephant Rocks by thetrackswetravel.com
Back cover image: Granny's Pool by Peter Hodgson
Book design by: Christine Schiedel and Cory Spence

CONTENTS

THE SOUTH WEST

Western Australia is the largest state in Australia. The region we call 'The Southwest' occupies only about a tenth of the area of the state and yet here lies the greatest variety of habitat. The floral diversity alone is one of the richest on the planet with over 7400 species found and counting: that's a lot of wildflowers.

The southwest geographic border is easily defined as it marks the edge of where our eucalypt woodlands give way to the endless mulga which in turn leads into our dryer deserts. It is also an important cultural divide: there is a distinct zone where the southwest Noongar people's land blends into other traditional indigenous lands. Travelling the southwest is relatively easy with a network of roads and tracks taking you to every corner within a day or so. The area is not considered remote (from Perth anyway), however with a relatively low population it allows the traveller to find many quiet places where stunning sandy beaches and cool forests can be all but deserted. All around the southern coastline to the Nullarbor cliffs there is a myriad of beautiful beaches and one only needs to venture a few kilometres inland and you can be standing amongst the giant Karri and Red Tingle trees where a world of mosses, fungi and bird calls awaits you. Heading also south takes you to a multitude of areas where vineyards, hill ranges and forests abound.

There truly is lots do and explore in this beautiful part of Australia.

Above: Thistle Cove in Cape Le Grand National Park, one of the many beautiful beaches found along the southern coastline. The further east one travels the greater the chances of finding secluded beaches, particularly in winter and spring.

Left: The delicate Scarlet mountain bell is found only in the Stirling Range. There are several species of mountain bell and most are found in this range, where each species grows in a very restricted area, some found only on the high altitudes, others on the lower slopes.

Following page: Driving through the tall Karri Forests gives us a humble sense of scale while at the same time bringing silence and peace so often needed in this hectic world. The Karri trees are not the tallest trees in Australia - the giant Mountain Ash in Tasmania takes that award - but the tallest Karri trees are thought to reach 90 metres and are not far behind.

THE SOUTH WEST

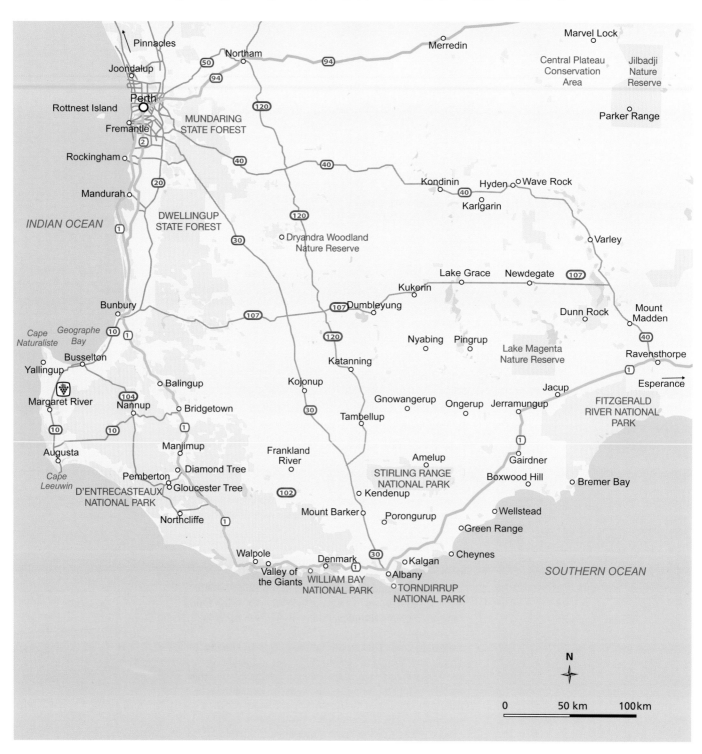

Pinnacles

Joondalup

50 Northam

94

Merredin

Marvel Lock

Central Plateau
Conservation
Area

Jilbadji
Nature
Reserve

Perth

Rottnest Island

Fremantle

MUNDARING
STATE FOREST

120

Parker Range

Rockingham

2

40

40

Mandurah

20

DWELLINGUP
STATE FOREST

Kondinin

Hyden

Wave Rock

40

Karlgarin

INDIAN OCEAN

1

30

120

Dryandra Woodland
Nature Reserve

Varley

Lake Grace

Newdegate

107

Bunbury

107

Kukerin

Dunn Rock

Mount
Madden

Cape
Naturaliste

Geographe
Bay

10

1

107

Dumbleyung

40

Busselton

120

Nyabing

Pingrup

Lake Magenta
Nature Reserve

Ravensthorpe

Yallingup

Katanning

1

Esperance

Balingup

Kojonup

Jacup

FITZGERALD
RIVER NATIONAL
PARK

Margaret River

104

Nannup

Gnowangerup

Ongerup

Jerramungup

Bridgetown

30

Tambellup

10

10

1

Frankland
River

1

Augusta

Manjimup

Amelup

Gairdner

Boxwood Hill

Bremer Bay

Cape
Leeuwin

Pemberton

Diamond Tree

102

STIRLING RANGE
NATIONAL PARK

D'ENTRECASTEAUX
NATIONAL PARK

Gloucester Tree

Kendenup

Wellstead

Northcliffe

1

Mount Barker

Porongurup

Green Range

Walpole

Denmark

30

Kalgan

Cheynes

SOUTHERN OCEAN

Valley of
the Giants

1

Albany

WILLIAM BAY
NATIONAL PARK

TORNDIRRUP
NATIONAL PARK

N

0   50 km   100km

GEOLOGY

The geology of the southwest has a complex history spread literally over aeons. When the massive supercontinent of Gondwanaland split into the tectonic plates of India, Australia and the Antarctic, it created a huge rift valley leaving predominantly granitic material. With time these materials were compressed and left as a huge granite mass known as the Achaean Yilgarn Craton, which underlays much of the southwest region. It is by far the largest granite block in Australia and one of the oldest. Overlaying much of the Yilgarn Craton are sedimentary rocks, the remnants of ancient seabeds formed long after the granites and quartz were formed. The resulting limestone deposits and windblown shell grains and quartz sands line much of the western coastline. Heading east from Perth, you leave the coastal limestone plain and climb up the steep Darling Scarp, which is the edge of the huge granite mass. Here it has a thick overlaying coating of laterite, from which comes bauxite, the primary mineral used in the manufacture of Aluminium.

Huge exposed granite domes are witness to the gigantic granite Yilgarn mass that lies below. As you head southwest into the large wheatbelt zone, you are mostly driving over sedimentary deposits, but you don't leave the granite outcrops behind: they are known as inselbergs and often have their own rich flora and fauna. On the outer margins of the Yilgarn Craton there are small mountain ranges created by the massive pressure inherent in drifting continents. The folds in the low hills expose beautiful banded ironstone rocks, which contain some of the richest iron ore deposits in the world. However, what the far eastern margins of the Yilgarn block are most noted for are the rich gold deposits that have created huge wealth for Western Australia for more than a century.

The wheatbelt is generally flat and roads cross ancient river valleys that have long lost their steep banks and now crisscross the country as a line of salt lakes. These ancient lakes systems are known as playa lakes.

Right: Part of the rock face of Bluff Knoll in the Stirling Range, known to the Noongar people as Koi Kyeunu-ruff. The mountain range consists of primarily metamorphic rocks: shales and quartzites. If you look in the foreground you can see a denser quartz vein.

Left: Part of the Leeuwin Naturaliste coastline north west of Margaret River. Here the hard granite gneiss (pronounced 'nice') ridge runs north-south with an overlay of limestone soils. All along the hinterland, not far from the coast, are deep limestone caves.

CLIMATE

The southwest has a Mediterranean Climate with generally wet winters and dry summers but it's a large area so winters in the deep southwest are wetter but generally not as cold as the outer wheatbelt, which in July can be colder but also have far less rain.

The further you head east or north from the coastline, the dryer the weather. If you are planning a tour in the southwest, late spring is ideal with temperatures averaging 27°C maximum. However, if you were wishing to see wildflowers in the Perth area, for example, late August to mid-September is a high point although there is more chance of experiencing rain.

Those who come to get away from cold weather and love the sun and beaches start appearing in mid-October. Be ready for hot days in summer take good skin care: sadly Australia has one of the highest rates of contracting skin cancer in the world so as we say, 'slip, slop, slap' with block out cream.

■ The weather varies substantially from north of Perth to way down south in the Walpole and Albany area. Towns like Albany rarely have temperatures above 30°C, even in mid-summer (although there will always be exceptional days and 45°C that far south is not unknown). A common problem for some visitors from overseas is thinking it won't get cold - it's wise to have that pullover packed just in case!

SUMMER

■ (December – March)
In the hottest driest season, with its occasional thunderstorms, expect temperatures of 30–40°C. The bush turns a range of brown colours and it's a testing time for wildlife with many species of birds flying to the wet tropics or retreating to the deep southwest.

AUTUMN

■ (April-May)
The big heat subsides and gives way to milder weather with the occasional rainy day. Expect a temperature range of 27–32°C. Some wildflowers start to bloom particularly those of the acacia family.

WINTER

■ (June – August)
It does feel cool, even cold, but rarely in the southwest does one experience temperatures below 5°C, except in the outer wheatbelt in the early hours of the day. The average is 15–25°C. Many days are beautifully sunny and lots species of wildflowers start to bloom, particularly from mid-August on. Perth locals will often head north to either the deserts, Pilbara or Kimberley for their holidays.

SPRING

■ (September – November)
A wonderful time of year with its many pleasant sunny days and warm temperatures (usually around 24–32°C). The bush becomes a blaze of colour particularly in species hot spots like the Stirling Range or the Fitzgerald River National Park.

PEOPLE

Above and right: With a wonderful Mediterranean climate, locals and visitors alike find great pleasure in our clear seas and vibrant beach life.

The indigenous Noongar people have been in the southwest of Australia for thousands of years. Estimates vary but it seems not unlikely that same cultural group have inhabited the region for upwards of 30,000 years, a tenure almost unrivalled outside of Australia. To say they knew the land is a vast understatement and although they cannot be said to have had no impact on the region, their impacts were mostly benign, well-managed and environmentally stable.

The Portuguese were the first Europeans to venture into these southern seas but the first to definitely come into southwest waters were the Dutch. The Eendracht, a flagship of the mighty Dutch East India Company, landed on these shores in 1616. The Dutch were to make land several times over the next hundred years or so, mainly on their route to Indonesia, and often as not accidentally. They had discovered it was quicker to utilize the strong trade winds below the equator once they had circumnavigated the Cape of Good Hope, come close to the coastline and then sail north, but unfortunately many ships were wrecked travelling this route on the many coral islands.

The small British brig, the Amity, under the command of Major Edmund Lockyer, entered the safe waters of King George Sound in Albany on the 9th November 1826. He took possession of the land, thus averting possible claims by the French. From here events were to unfold at a rapid rate. On the 2nd May 1829 Captain Charles Fremantle proclaimed that Western Australia would become a colony of the British Empire and a settlement on the Swan River - where Perth now lies - would be founded. Captain James Stirling was the governor and guided the Swan River settlement through the first difficult years.

Perth and the Southwest have now developed into a thriving and prosperous region and few realize how much of its wealth was founded by the hard work of those early settlers – and the unintentional and unwelcome sacrifice of its original inhabitants.

INDIGENOUS CULTURE

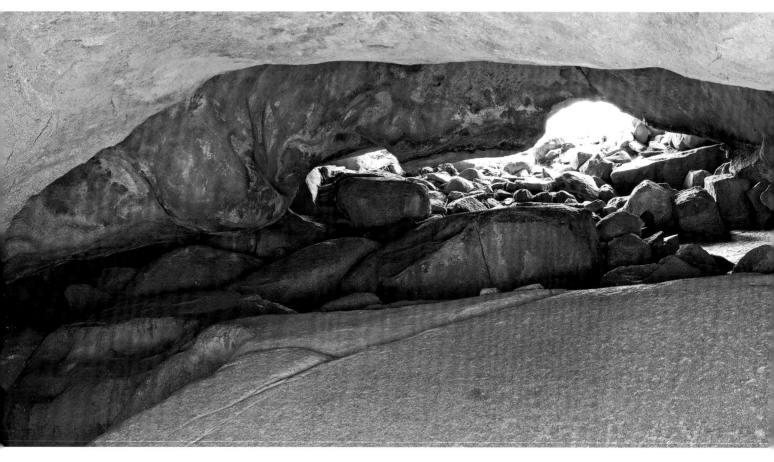

The Noongar people call the southwest 'Noongar boodjar', meaning 'Noongar Country', and what we call the southwest is almost identical to perimeters' of Noongar lands. So, if you travel north or the east of the southwest region, then you enter different very dialectical areas. The Noongar people have lived here in the southwest for at least 30,000 years according to archaeological records.

As with all Australian indigenous peoples there is no written language and so the word Noongar is often spelt as Nyoongar, Noongah or Nyunga. Their ancestral land covers one of the largest indigenous cultural blocks in Australia and within this region there are 14 what dialectical groups, once referred to as 'tribes'.

Earlier we discussed the European based climatic calendar, but the Noongar people see more subtle changes throughout the year and divide each year into six distinct periods. The first is 'Birak': roughly December and January, dry and hot. 'Bunuru': February to March, the hottest time. 'Djeran': April to May, the cooler weather begins. 'Makuru': June to July, the coldest and wettest period. 'Djilba': August to September, changing weather with some rain and warmer days. 'Kambarang': October to November, rains lessen and there are longer, drier days.

There are now approximately 21,000 people residing in the southwest who identify themselves as being a 'Noongar' person. Many live in country towns, particularly in the wheatbelt, and their rich culture and history is still being recorded.

Opposite page: Mulka's Cave located near the wheatbelt town of Hyden. This cave has a long-held mythology, important for the local Njakinjaki people who are part of the wider Nyoongar people. Normally a cave has just 5 to 10 markings or artwork; here there are over 300 markings, showing the significance of the cave.

Left: A clutch of Emu eggs were a favourite find for all indigenous people as the eggs supplied so much protein - but reading reports from early settlers, they rarely took all the clutch as the Noongar had formed their own ecological rules based on sheer practicality.

ECONOMY

Many are aware that the Pilbara, where mining dominates the economy, is one of the major economic regions of WA, but here in the southwest mining still contributes a large part of WA exports. The primary commodities exported are the rich bauxite deposits in the Darling Range, and mineral sands. The latter are not sands used for building materials but in the process of producing titanium. Australia is the largest exporter of mineral sands and WA exported $554 million worth in 2016-17. To put the economy of the state in real perspective, only a few years back Western Australia's export trade amounted to 46 % of Australia's total export value and the southwest was a large contributor.

Here in the southwest the Wheatbelt farmers harvest nearly half the wheat exported from Australia, and there are many other cereals produced in huge quantities including canola, barley, oilseed, lupins and oats. The southwest not only exports cereals but other commodities that can be a big surprise for visitors. For example, $48 million dollars' worth of carrots leave the state; even crops we assume are imported, such as strawberries actually have a net export.

The wine growing regions, particularly in the Margaret River area, produce some of the finest wines one can taste. Tourism plays an important role throughout the year but when the spring arrives, visitors from both the eastern states and overseas come to witness some of the finest displays of wildflowers to be found anywhere in the world.

Above: Storing wine in the traditional European Oak barrel is a real art: there are so many things to consider. Storage temperature must be maintained at around 12–13°C or 55°F (it's critical); and humidity must be equally controlled. Oak barrel ageing is an age-old tradition and gives either reds or whites their distinct flavours.

Left: Mustering sheep on a York farm. For this particular family, horses are their love so why not use them to muster?

Above: Huge granite boulders in the southwest Wheatbelt are the refuge for our rare Black-flanked Rock-wallaby.

Right: Western Spinebill.

Be it mammals, reptiles, insects, birds or bats the traveller can find a wealth of creatures throughout the region. In the mammal kingdom of the southwest the marsupial world dominates. They vary in size from the cute little Honey Possum to the big male Western Grey Kangaroo. Most are nocturnal although some, like the Honey Possum, can be sometimes be seen in the daytime scurrying up and down the banksia cones feeding on the flowers' nectar, and the Numbat is diurnal (out during daylight hours). Some, like the Red-tailed and Brush-tailed Phascogale are ferocious little killers that tackle creatures twice their size - but they are hard to see running fast through the sheoak woodlands.

In a world where the loss of our marsupials is commonplace, it is wonderful to hear when one is rediscovered. In the deep southwest at Two Peoples Bay the Gilbert's Potoroo was found in 1994. The English naturalist John Gilbert first discovered it in 1841 but even with extensive searches in the 1970s it was thought to be extinct. It is estimated there are less than 100 individuals in the wild, making it one of our rarest animals. Coincidentally another creature was rediscovered in the same area. This time it was not a marsupial but an almost flightless bird, the Noisy Scrub-bird - and noisy it is. It too was reduced to small numbers when first rediscovered but with good translocation programs in place the population now is far higher. Attention has now turned to protecting our rare Western Ground Parrot; a small breeding program is underway to help save this critically endangered bird.

Another rare animal still surviving on the larger granite domes in the wheatbelt is the attractive Black-flanked rock-wallaby, a very shy animal that comes out to feed from its rock shelters in the evening although in winter it will venture out longer throughout the day.

Luckily not everything is rare and there are many beautiful birds that the visitor can readily find. Some species can only be seen in the southwest like our stunning Red-capped Parrot or the huge Baudin's Black-Cockatoo found in the Jarrah forests. With a multitude of National Parks and reserves to visit there is so much wildlife to see.

■ Top: Brush-tailed Possum.

Above: Black-flanked Rock-wallaby.

WILDLIFE

On the western edge of the Wheatbelt between the towns of Narrogin and Williams lies the Dryandra Woodland Nature Reserve. In the 1960s this remnant patch of wandoo and gimlet woodland was about to be mined and the well-known ecologist Vincent Serventy fought long and hard to save the area from being cleared. Over the years it has become one of the last strongholds of some of our rare marsupials, not least the beautiful Numbat.

The Australian Geographic Society is a not-for-profit organization and true to its charter it awards well deserving Australians who have contributed to making our planet a better place. One category is for Australian Geographic Conservationists of the Year. In 2018 it was given to three individuals: John Lawson, Robert McLean and Sean Van Alphen. They share a great love for the environment and became passionate about the plight of the Numbat. They have now spent several years and thousands of volunteered hours helping protect it and its habitat from future loss, including combating a proposed rubbish disposal facility being created close to the Dryandra reserve. The campaign became the trigger to making the public aware of this latest possible impact on Numbat survival. Numbats feed exclusively on termites, extracting them with their extremely long tongue from subterranean passageways or from fallen logs where their acute smell finds the various termite runs. It's estimated that each Numbat requires about 20,000 termites a day to sustain them.

Besides the Numbat there are several other threatened animals still surviving in this small reserve including the Tammar Wallaby, Brush-tailed Bettong, Red-tailed Phascogale, Honey Possum, Western Pygmy Possum, Mardo and Chudtich. Also two uncommon birds, the Mallee Fowl and the Western Shriketit, and the beautiful Carpet Python.

Above Left: This is some of the last remaining wandoo where the endangered Numbat manages to survive (with strict feral fox and cat management controls).

From far left: Western Pygmy Possum, Brush-tailed Bettong, Thorny Devil, Numbat.

PLANTLIFE

If there is one thing that sets the southwest apart from all other regions of Australia, it would have to be its wealth of wildflowers. There are approximately 7300 species in the southwest: ironically, much of that diversity within the Wheatbelt region, where up to 90 % of the original vegetation has been cleared for farming. Scattered across the Wheatbelt are various reserves; as a rule, they are small but those in the east are a lot larger. All contain a wealth of species, some extremely rare and locally restricted. In particular, what is known as the Kwongan heath contains an amazing diversity of plants and is recognised as one of Earth's biodiversity-hotspots. The Kwongan soils are actually the most nutrient deficient in the southwest, so why is it so biologically rich? The southwest has been cut off from the rest of Australia, by dry regions such as the central deserts and Nullarbor Plain, for millions of years. The climate has been very stable during that time, leading in turn to a very stable, even if impoverished, environment. Plants have evolved into myriad different forms from their original parent stocks while competing for limited resources.

The flowering season starts early in the northern part of the southwest, as early as the end of July and builds up in numbers with a high point in late September. As one travels south, the richest time for wildflowers on the south coast is about mid-October. By the end of November wildflower numbers subside.

Mt Lesueur National Park, just north of Perth, has the single richest flora density with at least 900 species in a relatively small in area. Travelling south to the bigger parks like the Stirling Range and the Fitzgerald River National Park the numbers are staggering. There are at least 1800 flora species in the Fitzgerald: whatever month you come there will always be something in flower.

Top left: The stunning wildflower display in Dryandra Woodland Nature Reserve.

Above: Scarlet Banksia *Banksia coccinea*.

From left: Scallop Hakea *Hakea cucullate*, Wax Grevillea *Grevillea insignis*, Custard Orchid *Thelymitra villosa*.

Following page: The Kwongan heath east of Hyden in full bloom

PERTH

From the humble beginnings of the first colonial settlement founded in 1829, Perth has now developed into one of the largest cities in Australia with a population of just shy of 2 million and still growing. It is the most isolated city in Australia, and one of the most isolated on Earth (the nearest city of anything like a comparable size is Adelaide, 2500 kilometres away). It is the major centre for commerce and all the big mining companies have their head offices for the state located here.

Located on the banks of the Swan River, Perth is a pretty city and the view overlooking the city from Kings Park is always a favourite. On the west coast there are continuous sandy beaches running both north and south.

For those flying in from overseas or from the east coast the visitor can drive to any corner of the southwest in a day. It is only a short drive east to the Darling Range hills where many National Parks are located. There there are numerous walking trails and cycle tracks here - so much to do for the more adventurous. In the flower season the Darling Scarp is a blaze with colour during spring.

■ Left: Swan Valley wine region is a popular inland destination.

Above: The stunning cultural bridge at Elizabeth Quay in Perth

FREMANTLE AND

Fremantle is a vibrant place with markets, a maritime museum, arts centre, harbour, historical prison and lots of restaurants and cafés to enjoy. A leading international architectural historian once said that Fremantle was one of the finest colonial ports in the world; much has been restored and the blend of old and new makes for a delightful atmosphere.

It was occupied before Perth was established and is the main entry port for the city. In the early days, ships could not enter the harbour due to a limestone ridge that blocked the entrance to the Swan River, but the remarkable engineer C.Y. O'Connor solved that problem and by 1902 Fremantle had a harbour that could birth ocean-going liners.

Above: Fremantle Harbour is a perfect spot to wine and dine.

ROTTNEST ISLAND

Above: The Basin is a popular swimming bay on Rottnest Island.

Rottnest Island has long been a retreat for many Perth residents. Although only a few kilometres off the coast, after only a few hours on the island one becomes totally relaxed, like it's a million miles away. Blessed by a multitude of sandy beaches and clear and (generally) unpolluted shallow bays, it is an ideal place for swimmers and snorkelers. The underwater sea life here is rich and relatively undisturbed: sea horses, seals and many-coloured fish greet the diver once entering these clear waters. The cute little marsupial Quokka is common on the island and fairly tame - yet on the mainland is very uncommon. The name Rottnest came from the 'rats' nest', given by the early Dutch explorer Willem de Vlamingh when he saw so many Quokkas on the island. Ferry connections from Perth are frequent and there are many types of accommodation (balloted in high season!) for those who want to make a weekend or week of their visit.

BUSSELTON

Above: The 2-kilometre
long Busselton Jetty.

South of Perth on the west coast, the traveller might pass through the major towns of Rockingham, Mandurah and Bunbury which all have something to offer for the visitor. Just south of Mandurah, on Lake Clifton, there is a viewing walkway that juts out to the lake. The Thrombolites that can be seen here are almost unchanged descendants of some of Earth's earliest life forms. These small circular domes consist of layers calcium carbonate built up by the fine living film of bacteria on the top, examples of what the first living structures looked like some 3.5 billion years ago.

Busselton was named after the Bussell family who settled in 1834 on their cattle station Cattle Chosen. The town is located on Geographe Bay, named by the early French navigator and naturalist Nicholas Baudin when he sailed in these waters in 1801. Busselton's centre of attraction is its long timber jetty, the longest timber jetty in the southern hemisphere at nearly 2 kilometres long. It's so long that that there is a small tourist train that ferries people out to the end. You can also access an underwater observatory: the waters here are generally clear and pristine and a colourful gallery of sea creatures and flora inhabit the piers under the jetty.

Busselton is also considered to be the gateway to the Margaret River region with the first main tourist town of Dunsborough only a short distance south.

Above: The walkway out onto Lake Clifton that visits the ancient Thrombolites.

Below: Beautiful sea horses can be found in the seas of Western Australia.

Following page: Canal Rocks, south of Yallingup.

CAPE TO CAPE

The Cape to Cape region is a truly wonderful part of Western Australia, with so many things the visitor can do. The rugged sea cliffs and many pristine beaches make it a must-do on many visitors' bucket lists: over half a million visitors come to the region each year. One of the most spectacular walks in the country can be taken between Cape Naturaliste in the north to Cape Leeuwin in the south where you can walk high above the coastline and then drop down behind pristine beaches. There are several places close to track where the visitor can stay and take a break. This coastline is also noted for its wonderful surf breaks and international surfing events are held here every year.

The inland region between the capes is home to over 200 wineries, some of international standing. Many provide wonderful lunches alongside their wine tasting facilities. Driving down the coastal road there are numerous other detours that lead to a variety of distractions, such as many galleries displaying art and sculpture work - and it's only a short drive to Cape Naturaliste with its old lighthouse (and more beaches). There are also over 200 limestone caves, of which 6 are open to the public offering self-guided audio tours enhancing the visitor's experience. Some of the caves contain fossils dating back 35,000 years.

Above: The crystal-clear waters of Smiths Beach on a calm day south of Yallingup.

Far left: The magnificent coastal walk from Cape Naturaliste to Cape Leeuwin.

Left: World class waves break off the Margaret River coast.

MARGARET RIVER

Nestled in the heart of the Cape to Cape region, Margaret River is the core town of the region and central to many of the wineries. It also has fine galleries, many showcasing entrancing wood furniture designs, all made from the beautiful local timbers of jarrah, marri and sheoak. The main tourist centre is professional slick centre giving the best advice to those visiting. They know all the local tours available and what wineries are open to the public.

The history of wine growing in Margaret River is really remarkable considering the first serious wineries did not start until the late 1960s. The region may be relatively new, but it soon showed its potential. Wine distributors and buffs quickly became aware that this was a region to keep a close eye on and it is now ranked as one of the Australia's best wine growing areas. Even though Margaret River wines contribute only 3-4 % of the annual Australian tonnage, the area supplies 20% of Australia's premium wines. Many vineyards would be classed as boutique wineries, but the larger vineyards produce about 8000 tonnes a year. One of the major reasons why the wines are so successful is the almost perfect Mediterranean climate, very similar to that in the classic wine growing region of Bordeaux. Interestingly most of the first growers were amateurs from the medical profession. Both red and white varieties are grown here, however the largest variety crushed is Sauvignon Blanc.

South of Margaret River, adjacent to Cape Leeuwin, is the small town of Augusta. Smaller than Margaret River, it still has all the major facilities that a holiday maker would wish for and close to the southern beaches. At Hamelin Bay the stingrays are very tame and just swim around your feet: yes they can be deadly creatures but here they are not so harmful when people stand in knee high water.

Left: Karri trees in the Boronup Forest south of Margaret River.

Top: Wine tasting is a popular activity for visitors.

Above: Vineyards along Caves Road.

Following page: The swimming area at Grannys Pool near Augusta.

TALL FOREST COUNTRY

Here in the deep southwest Karri trees can reach heights of around 90 metres, making the species one of the tallest in the world, although here in Australia the Tasmanian Mountain Ash is a little taller. The public have the opportunity to climb some of the tall Karri trees, including the Gloucester Tree, Diamond Tree and Dave Evans Tree, as they were used for fire-spotting and sport basic ladders to platforms in the upper reaches. The region was timber mill country, cutting millions of tons of forest logs. In the 1920s one mill had a contract to cut half a million railway sleepers for the Trans-Australian Railway. Also, some of Sydney's early roads had Karri paving as a base.

When Perth experiences high temperatures in mid-summer, many venture south to the cooler wet forests. The thick understorey retains more moisture than open country, which makes for a cooler environment full of the smells of the many plants, like the Karri Hazel, which grow in the deep Karri loam soils. The six major towns in the tall forest region all have festivals or attractions. Bridgetown hosts a famous Blues Festival; Nannup both music and flower festivals, and bike event; Manjimup has a top motorcross event; Pemberton has a leading mountain bike and cycle race; and Walpole has a sailing event!

The famous long Bibbulman Track passes right through this country on its way to the coast from Perth. From Northcliffe it's a short drive to Windy Harbour where there are views across the Southern Ocean. South of Pemberton 4WDrivers head to the remote coastline in D'Entrecasteaux National Park where some of the tallest inland sand dunes in the southern hemisphere await the intrepid off-road driver. Last, but not least, there are a multitude of remote campsites awaiting families who wish to experience the solitude of tall forest country.

Above: Many tourists love climbing the giant tall Karri Trees.

Left: A clearing near Walpole giving beautiful views to the coast though the Karri forest.

VALLEY OF THE GIANTS

Walpole receives the highest rainfall in Western Australia - about 1200 mm per annum – and on the south coast near Walpole and Denmark are the last remnant wet forests that once covered a far greater area. They now cover just 6000 hectares, the realm of the giant Tingle trees, relics of wetter times and the oldest living eucalypts in Australia. There are three Tingle tree species: Red Tingle, Yellow Tingle and Rate's Tingle. The Red Tingle grows the tallest (up to 75 metres), however it is the buttress that really impresses: they can have girth of 24 metres. The Ancient Empire Walk at the Valley of the Giants, not far from Walpole, puts our diminutive size in perspective: you can literally walk through some of the giant buttresses as wildfires have created huge hollows. As with many eucalypts most of the nutrients and fluids these giants need flow up the outer layers of their trunks and the trees still stand tall. To really appreciate these beautiful trees, take the elevated tree top walk through the canopy. The gateway to these walks is the information centre, providing a wealth of information on the trees and their environment.

Around Walpole there are many other picturesque areas to visit, including Fernhook Falls, Circular Pool, Conspicuous Cliffs and Mandalay Beach. Close to the town is a lovely drive around the Walpole Inlet and the opportunity to take an eco-cruise boat trip to the entrance of the bay. If you really want to get a feeling of how extensive the southern forests are then a drive to Mount Frankland – a hike up will reveal all, but the climb is for reasonably fit people only: from the base of this huge granite there's a steep track and finally a climb up an enclosed ladder to the very top and the perfect 360 degree view.

Above: Over time fires can burn through the centre of trees but as long as the outer membrane of the bark is intact the tree will still live and support itself.

Top right: Part of the lovely walkway that wanders through the big buttressed Tingle trees in the Valley of the Giants.

Bottom right: The high walkway that takes walkers up into the canopy of the Karri trees.

AROUND DENMARK

The drive along the south coast highway to Denmark is very scenic and there are many glorious beaches. Just south of the highway, in William Bay National Park, are the delightful Greens Pool and Elephant Rocks. The swimming here is relatively safe because huge boulders break the force of the Southern Ocean waves. Around the bay is another picturesque bay: Madfish Bay. 4WDrivers often head further down to Boat Harbour Road to a beautiful – and much less busy - coastline. Ocean Beach is the closest to town and is a classic surfing beach, with lessons available. Further east is Lights Beach a local favourite: the sunsets from here can be absolutely breathtaking.

Denmark was settled soon after the Great War by people under what was known as the Soldier Settlement Scheme. They were hard years for those trying to open up the tall forests country and make a living, and the town still holds to its salt-of-the -earth character. Denmark has drawn artists from all over Australia so the visitor can see artwork and sculptures either in town in the many small galleries that are dotted around the countryside. They are complemented by folk concerts that run through much of the year.

Left: The gigantic granite boulders near Green Pool aptly named Elephant Rocks.

Above: Green Pool near Walpole is a favourite with many visitors as the bay is protected by many submerged rocks that lay just off the beach line making it safer for families.

Following page: Ocean Beach is only a short distance from Denmark and a favourite with surfers.

THE STIRLING RANGE

Left: The view from Bluff Knoll looking west through the Stirling Range.

Below: The steel walkway high up in the Porongurup Range.

& THE PORONGURUPS

From the flat plains of the southern wheatbelt the beautiful peaks of the Stirling Range rise abruptly to the sky. Known to the Koreng Noongar people as Koi Kyeunu-ruff. In geological terms the mountain range is relatively young, only forming about 1.2 million years ago and consisting primarily of sedimentary rocks, mainly sandstone, greenschist, quartzite, shale and slate. High in the range are examples of ancient seabeds that have been thrust above the surrounding plain. The geology is totally different to the extremely old granite of the Yilgarn Craton which these sedimentary rocks overlay. The Stirling Range National Park encompasses most of the range and there are many walking trails to the various peaks. The most popular being the climb up Bluff Knoll, which normally takes 3–4 hours. Needless to say there are panoramic 360-degree views from the summit of this 1099-metre high mountain.

The range is home to an extremely dense diversity of flora: one of the highest in Western Australia with 1500 species (more flowering plants than are found in the whole of the British Isles). Due to the ranges higher altitude compared with the surrounding flat plains, it experiences its own climate, allowing distinct species to develop over time: one reason the range has over 80 species found nowhere else in the world. The beautiful mountain bells are a wonderful example of this: some of the species of bells are found only on single peaks.

To really appreciate the beauty of this 60-kilometre range there is a well graded dirt road, the Stirling Range Drive, that runs through the heart of the entire range. Expect great photographic opportunities and several quiet picnic spots along the way. Just south of the Stirlings is another range, the Porongurups. The climate is slightly cooler and the soil quite different, allowing the most easterly Karri trees to grow here. The geology is also quite different as the range consists of great granite outcrops.

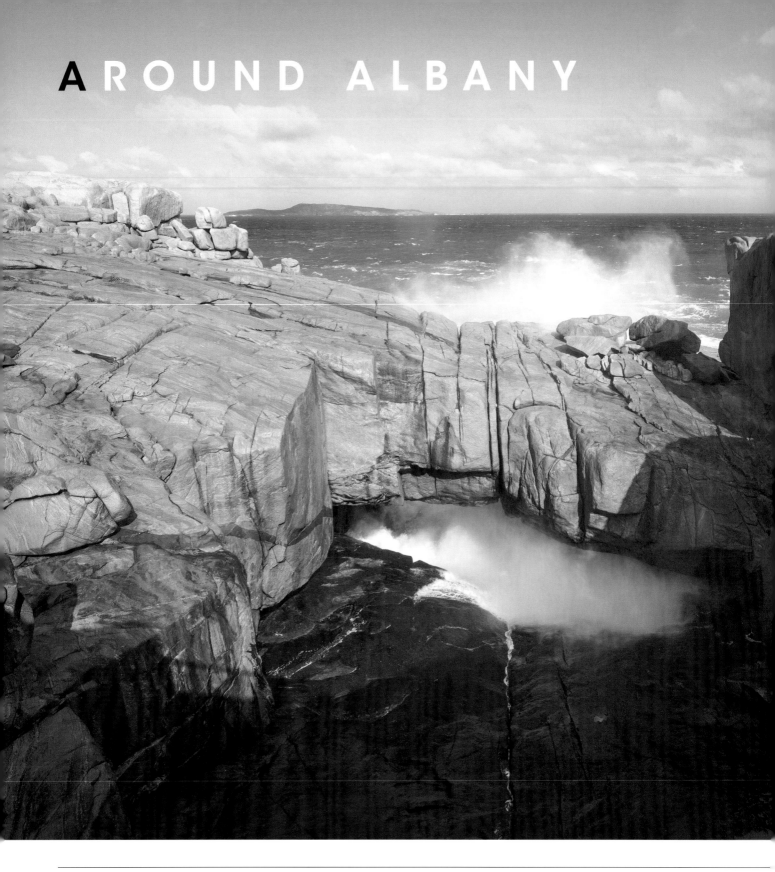

A lbany was settled by the British before Perth was established, although both the Dutch and French had explored this coastline previously and even American whaling ships had visited these shores in bygone times. There is a replica of the small brig, the Amity, commanded by Edmund Lockyer who first established a penal settlement in December 1826. In an age when many wrongs were committed against the First Australians, it is refreshing to hear a good deed story. Lockyer must have been a man of high moral standing for he rescued a group of indigenous women from one of the islands in the bay who were being used as sexual slaves by some whalers. The whalers were subsequently shipped to the east coast to stand trial. The local Minang people held a corroboree in Lockyer's honour and there was a good relationship between the indigenous people and the Europeans for the first years of settlement.

Albany has a large, protected harbour and overlooking the bay on Mount Clarence is a world-class facility, the National Anzac Centre, commemorating the departure of 41,000 troops and military support staff (men and women) who converged on and departed Albany in 1914 to go and fight in the Great War. The centre shows the history and locations of the many ships that departed these shores.

A short drive from Albany town centre is Torndirrup National Park. The most popular features in the park are the Gap and Natural Bridge, formations in the granite cliffs. The constant pounding of the large waves of the Sothern Ocean have warn away the granite, taking advantage of the many cracks in the hard rock and creating huge crevices. Steel walkways jut out over the edge making it a breath tacking experience.

Left: The Natural Bridge in Torndirrup National Park.

Above: Displays at the National Anzac Centre.

FITZGERALD RIVER

f the Stirling Range's floral extravagance sounded impressive, the Fitzgerald River National Park surpasses it. Over 1800 species have been counted here; however, the park is about three times the size of the Stirlings, so perhaps that is to be expected.

Along the 90-kilometre coastline there are several ranges of hills: one is called the Barren Ranges but barren they certainly are not having a wealth of flora. The west sections of the park have graded tracks to West Mount Barren; there is walking track to the summit with views over the ocean and surrounding park and close by a track to Point Ann. Between July and early October there is a good chance of seeing the Southern Right Whale: they give birth and attend their young in the bay. The central part of the coastline has no vehicular access and is set aside for walkers only. This remote trail covers many kilometres and requires backpacks and sleeping gear.

At the eastern part of the Fitzgerald River Park there are even more opportunities to venture to secluded beaches and Hamersley Drive shows off the flora diversity of the park. Perhaps the most spectacular part is just below East Mount Barren, overlooking the ocean and the small town of Hopetoun. For even more magnificent views climb East Mount Barren past the tall Royal Hakea plants and the lovely Barrens Regalia lining the quartzite track.

NATIONAL PARK

Above: The view from East Mount Barren looking west across the Fitzgerald National Park.

Far left: The pendulous Lemanns Banksia.

Left: Barrens Regelia, only found on the eastern ranges.

Following page: Near Hamersley Inlet in the Fitzgerald National Park.

AROUND ESPERANCE

Esperance is the last major town on the south coast, about 710 kilometres southeast of Perth. Here are some of the bluest, clearest waters and whitest beaches in the State. Twilight and Blue Haven beaches are wonderful examples and very close to town. Off the coast are many islands and boat trips leave the central jetty to take visitors to Woody Island and Middle Island with its incredible pink lake, Lake Hillier. Surfers love this coastline as well as sun seekers although the Margaret River coast generally has bigger waves. Many beaches allow 4WD access and the area is considered a beach fisherman's paradise. Close by is Cape Le Grand National Park which has a few camping locations. In the height of the summer holidays farmers as well as other visitors take time out from the busy cropping season, taking a well-earned break. Some visitors walk up to the caves on Frenchman's Peak, others swim at Lucky Bay or Hellfire Bay.

Above: Overlooking the town of Esperance.

Left: The White-bellied Sea Eagle is seen occasionally along these shores.

Top left: Blue Haven Beach, just west of Esperance.

E ast of Esperance off the southern coastline are over a hundred islands and 1500 of what are known as islets, small rock islands but large enough to sink a ship if hit. The islands are known as the Recherche Archipelago and are managed by Western Australia's National Parks. These islands stretch for 240 kilometres east of Esperance and were first named by the French navigator Antoine Bruni d'Entrecasteaux. Archaeologists have found artefacts on the islands dating back 13,000 years and it's thought that the islands were connected to the mainland until a few thousand years ago. New Zealand Fur Seals and Australian Sea Lions live on many of the islands and both the Southern Wright and the Humpback Whales migrate through these waters. Both Sea Eagles and Cape Barren Geese are common throughout the Archipelago. On the mainland is the remote Cape Arid National Park, studded with beaches, good camp sites and rich in flora.

Top left: Near Taragon Bay in Cape Arid National Park.

Bottom left: Overlooking Hammer Head east of Esperance.

Below: Just a few of the one hundred plus islands in the Archipelago of the Recherche.

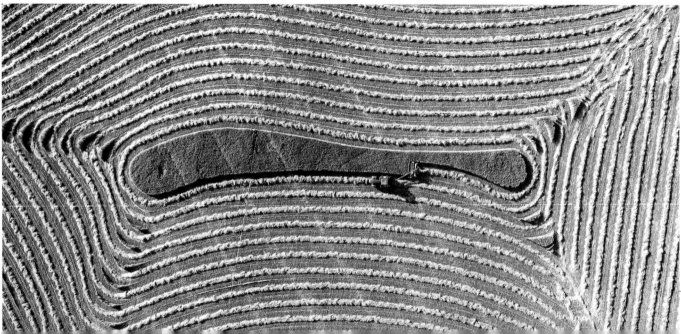

W A V E   R O C K

The Wheatbelt covers the largest portion of the southwest and even though wheat fields dominate the countryside, there is much to see. The old towns like York and Toodyay are relatively close to Perth but still retain many original buildings, examples of the first European settlement. Many of their residents are in fact descendants of the original European and indigenous families who settled here. There are many precious nature reserves that dot the region and they are havens for some of rich flora that once dominated most of this region, still one of the floristically richest areas in Western Australia.

A drive to Wave Rock and the Humps near the town of Hyden is popular with many visitors. Throughout the Wheatbelt there are many more granite outcrops that retain their flora and fauna. Hang-gliding and ballooning are favourite hobbies for many thanks to the consistent thermals, and people drive out from Perth to the inner wheatbelt to experience the joys of the air.

Top left: Patterns from the air on a farm near York.

Far left: Harvest time.

Top: Wave Rock near Hyden.

Left: Aerial photograph of wheat crop and wandoo trees near the town of York.

Following page: The late evening sun bursts through the grasstrees in the inner wheatbelt.

ACKNOWLEDGEMENTS

The Author would like to thank all the talented photographers, especially my fellow photographic friends Melody Chipper, Peter Hodgson, Willi Laufmann and Alex Graham. Many thanks to Jess Teidman of Australian Geographic for being helpful with the picture retrieval. I'd like to also thank Tourism Western Australia for allowing us to share some of their photographs, and to Katrina O'Brien and Andrew Swaffer, the main driving forces behind this series of Australian Geographic books. Finally a big thank you to designer Christine Schiedel for doing a fantastic job laying up and translating my rough ideas.

ABOUT THE AUTHOR

Although born in the UK, Simon Nevill has spent most of his life in Australia. He ran tours for over 20 years, taking clients overseas and to every state in Australia including all the main desert regions of this vast country. Initially an expert birder, he's developed a keen interest in wildflowers and other groups of the animal kingdom. He now has an extensive knowledge of Western Australia and enjoys sharing his photography, passion and knowledge with others.

ABOUT THE PUBLISHERS

The Australian Geographic journal is a geographical magazine founded in 1986. It mainly covers stories about Australia - its geography, culture, wildlife and people - and six editions are published every year. Australian Geographic also publish a number of books every year on similar subjects for both children and adults. A portion of the profits goes to the Australian Geographic Society which supports scientific research as well as environmental conservation, community projects and Australian adventurers. www.australiangeographic.com.au

Woodslane Press are a book publishing company based in Sydney, Australia. They are the publishers of Australia's best-selling walking guides and under their co-owned Boiling Billy imprint also publish camping, bush exploration and 4WD guides. For more than a decade committed to publishing books that empower Australians to better explore and understand their own country, Woodslane Press is proud to be working with Australian Geographic to produce this new series of souvenir books.

Also available:

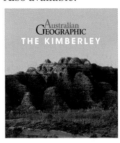  

PICTURE CREDITS

pi: Australian Geographic/Marie Lochmann
pii: Simon Nevill
p1:   John Lawson
p2-3:   Australian Geographic/Marie Lochmann;
         Simon Nevill
p5:   Melody Chipper
p6:   Australian Geographic/Jiri Lochmann
p7:   Simon Nevill
p9:   Australian Geographic
p10:   Australian Geographic/Andrew Gregory
p11:   Australian Geographic/Andrew Gregory
p12:   Simon Nevill
p13:   Simon Nevill
p14:   Tourism Western Australia
p15:   Melody Chipper
p16-7:   John Lawson (main image);
         Simon Nevill (others)
p18-9:   John Lawson
p20-1:   Simon Nevill (all images)
p22-3:   Simon Nevill
p24-5:   Tourism Western Australia (main image);
         Simon Nevill

p26:   Tourism Western Australia
p27:   Australian Geographic/Andrew Gregory
p28:   Alex Graham
p29:   Peter Hodgson (top);
         Australian Geographic/Justin Gilligan
p30-1:   Simon Nevill
p32:   Tourism Western Australia (bottom)
p32-33: Simon Nevill
p33:   Australian Geographic/
         David Dare Parker (bottom)
p34:   Alex Graham
p35:   Tourism Western Australia
         (top and bottom)
p36-7:   Peter Hodgson
p38:   Tourism Western Australia
p39:   Simon Nevill
p40:   Simon Nevill
p41:   Simon Nevill;
         Tourism Western Australia (bottom right)
p42:   Simon Nevill
p43:   Alex Graham
p44-5:   Simon Nevill

p46:   Australian Geographic/Jiri Lochmann
p47:   Australian Geographic/Jiri Lochmann
p48:   Peter Hodgson
p49:   Tourism Western Australia
p50-1:   Simon Nevill (all images)
p52-3:   Simon Nevill
p54:   Peter Hodgson
p55:   Simon Nevill (top);
         Peter Hodgson (bottom)
p56:   Simon Nevill (both images)
p57:   Australian Geographic/David Dare Parker
p58:   Melody Chipper (both images)
p59:   Melody Chipper (both images)
p60-1:   Simon Nevill
Rear cover: Peter Hodgson